HOW TO SAVE MONEY

ACTION INVESTING

DAN PAUL

Take Action Now

Click on the link below to connect to an infinite number of free books for review.
Sign up for a BookSprout membership and get free access to review copies.
Become a member of the Advance Review Copy Team called "ALT Review Team Supreme", a group of reviewers who specialize in reviewing books by Dan Paul. Become a lifetime member of an elite group of mastermind intellectuals who transform philosophy into action.

Step 1. Sign up for Booksprout.
Step 2. Read a book and leave a review on Amazon (requires spending $50/year on your Amazon account)

Sign up for ALT Review Team Supreme
Click on the link below.

https://booksprout.co/reviewer/team/60346/alt-review-team-supreme

CONTENTS

NOT WANTING

TAKE INACTION

Change Your Mind, Not Reality

The best way to save money is to practice not wanting.

- Stop craving anything, including possessions and lifestyles. Think about all the time it takes to store, maintain, and dispose of all of your possessions. What would you rather be doing?
- Utilize mind training, meditation, hypnosis, and setting goals to focus, organize, and achieve your objectives.

I don't want anything. Everything is a hassle. I do not want to store it, fix it, look at it, think about it, see it, hear it, feel it, or imagine that it is mine. I want freedom from want. I overdosed on the system. I have too much stuff. The clutter in the room is in my mind, and I can't focus or get anything done. I'm stuck in a field of too much.

My brain has been pummeled with messages that consumption, cars, money, and drinks will bring freedom;

however, who would want to be an indentured servant to the system? If I control my mind, I control my spending. I want to resist a system of domination of the air, land, water, plants, animals, and people. I would like to actively de-escalate, find solutions, and sustain without domination and oppression, which is inherent in the system and myself as a part of it. Yes, I was born of privilege and disadvantage, compared to whom? And some who faced enormous challenges, burdens, and disadvantages were much better prepared for life than those with advanced degrees and high-paying jobs.

Click the link below to receive free review copies of all the books listed below. To receive review copies, you must sign up for BookSprout and then read and review the books. The time to take action is now; click the link below to read and review my books.

https://booksprout.co/reviewer/team/60346/ad-supreme

The QR codes below link you to Amazon, where you can buy the e-book ($5) or paperback ($10).

The ollowing books were written by Dan Paul. These are the first five books in a series called Philosophy of Action Design and Multiplicity.

Auto Free Design

Workers Health Handbook

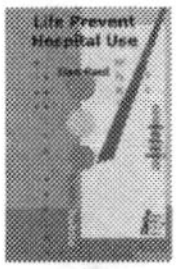

Save Your Life Prevent Hospital Use

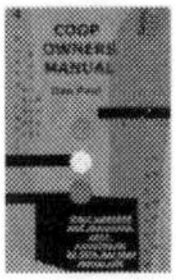

Coop Owners Manual

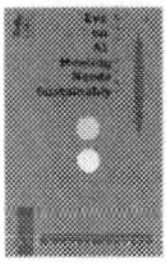

Eye on AI Meeting Needs Sustainably

The following books were written by Dan Paul. These are the second five books (5-10) in a series called Philosophy of Action Design and Multiplicity.

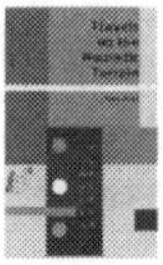

Travels on the Nomadic Terrain

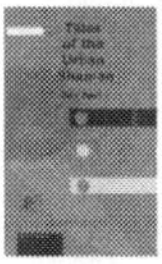

Tales of the Urban Shaman

Housing in the Danger Zone

Corona Time

Philosophy of Design, Action, and Multiplicity

The following books were written by Dan Paul.

Auto Free USA

AI Frankstein Concise, Critical, Common Sense Artificial Intelligence

Universal Voting System

Forever Flowers Requiem in the Land of Milk and Honey

Universal Basic Income

These books were written by Dan Paul.

Blueprint to Reverse Climate Change

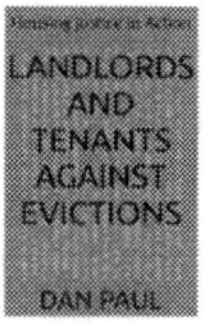

Landlords and Tenants Against Eviction

CHAPTER 1
HEALTHCARE

The Quagmire, I Need It, But I Can't Pay.

So you want to live to 150, really? Some people will do anything to avoid going to the hospital. Other people don't care about saving money or reducing spending, so they do what they want. The standard formula for a long life without using a hospital is the following:

- Eat whole foods and avoid all meat products.
- Exercise daily, and build your strength.
- Practice stress reduction and control.
- Set daily goals to practice safety throughout the day.

You can't control anyone or anything, so something will likely happen, and you will need to use the hospital. If you live in the United States, you may receive a substantial bill that you will have to pay for the rest of your life. If you have health insurance, it may or may not cover the costs. If you have no money, the hospital is required to help you.

. . .

How Can Eating Whole Foods Save Money?

Diet: Eating whole foods, carrots, potatoes, onions, rice, beans, and greens significantly reduces your chances of dying from the most likely causes of death, including heart disease, stroke, cancer, and diabetes. If you eat meals at home, you will avoid spending a lot of money on takeout and restaurant meals. One operation could cost a lifetime's worth of groceries so that prevention will save you the most money.

How Can Exercise Save Me Money?

Exercise: Adopting a simple exercise plan can improve your health, enabling you to live a long life and avoid the most common causes of death. A simple strategy is to walk for 30 to 60 minutes a day and do strength-building exercises.

How Can I Build Muscle Without Spending Money?

Common exercises like push-ups, pull-ups, sit-ups, knee bends, and bicycle crunches can help build your core and more, but be cautious. If you push it too hard, you will injure yourself. Begin with the least strenuous muscle building and gradually increase the amount of stress on your body. Engaging in regular exercise and strength training can help you save money by reducing your risk of injuries from falls or accidents. If you are sick, strength-building exercises may help you recover.

How Can Stress Reduction Help Me Save Money?

Making decisions is an essential way to save money. Your brain functions at its highest level when you are in a state of relaxation. Peak brain function may happen at the moment when you are barely awake and nearly asleep. If you avoid making decisions when you are too excited, you may figure out the best outcome for everyone involved, especially yourself. You will also be in a position to make a solution that will cost you the least amount of money. Controlling your stress through meditation and breathing can help you avoid situations that could lead to injury or disease infection. In the morning, I review potential stressful situations and devise ways to prevent conflict, and practice de-escalation to minimize the risk of injury or illness.

How Can Making Goals Help Me Save Money?

Your mind provides the best opportunity to save money. If you practice not wanting anything, you will not have a desire to spend money; instead, you will focus on getting what you want without spending money. Of course, this requires effort, and if you're not willing to put in the work, it's unlikely you will achieve results. If you make a plan not to spend money in the next five minutes, five hours, or five days, you are more likely to accomplish that goal. I can wake up in the morning and make a list of all the things I want to spend money on, and then figure out how to get what I want without spending money. Think of all the time it takes to buy, maintain, store, and dispose of an item. You may decide that it's not worth the effort. If I practice not wanting anything, the list would be tiny, and it wouldn't be so challenging to minimize my spending. If you set goals to avoid spending money in the morning and at night, and meditate on them, you will likely achieve those goals.

The old-fashioned way.

Many people lack health insurance. Some of them are aware that visiting a hospital can generate numerous problems, so they avoid going to the hospital. For healthy individuals, this can work if you are very careful; however, unforeseen circumstances can arise, and the dangers now are different from those 50 years ago. If you are very careful and lucky, perhaps this has worked for you, but it is very risky. You can wind up with a bill so large that you would have to declare bankruptcy or move to a country that prioritizes its people's well-being.

The Following Books By Dan Paul Help People Advance Their Healthcare.

Click on the blue text link below to buy the book on Amazon.

. . .

Workers Health Handbook

Workers Health Handbook

Save Your Life Prevent Hospital Use

Save Your Life Prevent Hospital Use

CHAPTER 2
HOUSING

How Can I Save Money On Housing Costs?

- Be flexible and helpful enough to live with anyone, anywhere, under any conditions.
- Generate money and skills to own, operate, manage, and fix housing.
- Live where other people don't want to live.
- Set housing goals frequently.

Be Flexible And Helpful.

If you train your mind to do whatever is needed to sustain a household, you are likely to be welcome at any time. Many people will avoid tasks like unclogging a toilet, cleaning the dishes, and organizing a mess. If you train your mind, you can easily do these things. If you are flexible enough to sleep on the floor, help with whatever is needed, and make the housing arrangement work, you may be able to reduce your housing costs. You could imagine yourself as the universal fix-it person. Of course, this has its disadvantages, but if you have a larger goal, it may be a necessary step in the process. Once you have more money, you'll have more options.

I Have No Money, There's No Way I Can Get Housing.

Many households have an extra bedroom, couch, or cabin. Some would be happy to have someone who can fix the door, take out the dog, cook some food, take out the garbage, and smile on demand. Of course, your mind would be ready to jump at the chance. If your specialty is to do nothing, this probably won't work. Another option is to make your shelter or find one that no one else is using. If you have many of these skills, that could be an option. I know squatters who have done very well, but had to endure harsh living conditions.

Develop Skills

In many communities, individuals with skills in carpentry, plumbing, or electrical work can make a significant contribution. If you can solve any problem, you have high value. In co-op housing, members own, manage, and operate the building in which they live. They must make sure it is up to code. If your building is up to code, the city building department cannot issue a violation. It's possible to minimize the repair bills by doing the work yourself. This is sweat equity, which presents a significant opportunity in a cooperative. The work must be done up to code. You may want to renovate a building. Find a decent building that needs renovation and add tremendous value.

Live Where You Can

Some say, "You do what you gotta do." Others live in cars, vans, trucks, boxes, mobile homes, under freeways, subways, and buildings. Living in a barn, hut, lean-to, A-frame, or similar structure can be challenging, but if it's in a community or in great weather, perhaps the quality of the housing isn't a significant issue. If all you need is a bedroom, since you can use the nearby kitchen or bathroom, you may be able to make the best of it.

Set Housing Goals

Without a goal, many people feel lost. Once you set a goal, you can move to achieve it. Create a to-do list to help you reach your goal. Ask other people about the limitations of your goal and adjust it if that will help you reach your goal. Make goals for one minute, 10 minutes, 10 hours, 10 days, 10 weeks, 10 months, 10 years, and the rest of your life. Just go through the process. If you do it frequently enough, you will become attached to the goal and establish a method to achieve it.

Join A Co-op

• • •

Many co-ops offer housing for 20-50% less than market-rate housing. You pay a security deposit, one month's rent, and an additional $150 per month, roughly, for food. Typically, members attend a weekly meeting, complete their work, and pay monthly to secure a decent place to live. You get a room and access to large common areas. Many co-ops include a space to work on your bicycle or fix the building, laundry facilities, and a garden..

The Following Books By Dan Paul Help People Advance Their Housing.

Click on the blue text link below to buy the book on Amazon.

Landlords and Tenants Against Eviction

Landlords and Tenants Against Eviction

Housing in the Danger Zone

Housing in the Danger Zone

CHAPTER 3
EDUCATION

How Can We Save Money When We Educate Ourselves?

Begin your education by setting goals for income, housing, healthcare, education, and transportation. Write down where you want to be in one month, 10 months, two years, and five years. How do you want to make money, and what kind of housing do you want? What income do you want? It may take time to identify your goals. Who inspires you? What inspires you about them? What goals did they set to get where they are? Your education is self-directed. It's tailored to exactly what you want; you don't take a bunch of courses that are largely irrelevant to your life. So write down what your goals are, how much money you want to make, where you want to live, and what kind of housing you want. Keep asking questions and reviewing your answers until it is clear that you are ready to commit, take action, and focus 100% on achieving your goal.

. . .

Make A List Of Wants:

- Healthcare, housing, education, transportation, and food.
- I want to live in a co-op with 10 other people.
- I want to live alone in a small apartment.
- I want to live in a family.
- I want to live in a community.

Make many lists of wants and read and meditate and rank your desires until you find one or two or three that you like the most. Continue this practice day after day, and keep a journal. You may forget the process if you don't look it over every month or two. This is akin to a sacred list that you are willing to devote all your energy to. Once you reach that point, you will be so motivated that you will get these things done very quickly.

Compose and Design: How to Save Money.

Only you can achieve your goal. It must be tailored to your specific circumstances; otherwise, you risk going in the wrong direction and having to start over. If your goal is to save money, what does that mean? Do not spend the money unless there is no other option. So the default is to solve the problem using what is here and now.

Free Education

. . .

The Internet provides information about anything you can think of; however, it means nothing if you are not motivated, do not have a direction, and do not have the discipline to carry out your mission. Mindset is crucial. You must train your mind or you'll get nowhere.

How to do this?

Set Measurable Goals.

- I will make $5000 a month with passive income in three years.
- I will spend money only if there is no other option for three years.
- I will make 10 paintings per month and two books.
- I will renovate one junker building per year.

Commit To It.

Often, it takes 2 to 5 years of intense work to establish a successful business.

No one else can do the work for you.

No excuses, no BS, no blaming.

Most people who pursue this path make numerous mistakes, face setbacks, and must persevere, often without earning a living for a prolonged period, sometimes for years.

Slowly, you will see results if you put in the time.

Mindset is crucial. If you give up after failing 100 times, you may not make it.

• • •

Some say, What does this have to do with education?

Many people struggle with the value of an education, especially when they go into debt and become an indentured servant to capitalism. Some individuals are required to repay student loans for the remainder of their lives. Many classes have no practical relevance. They will not assist you in obtaining healthcare, housing, education, transportation, or food. Additionally, many students are unclear about the purpose of their studies or the relevance of learning about medieval Europe. This is why another approach may be beneficial. If you ground your education in what is necessary, your motivation to study and develop your skills will improve, and the critical component of learning—motivation—will not be an abstract idea, but an absolute necessity. You will be more motivated to learn if you're learning is directly related to your goals.

CHAPTER 4
TRANSPORTATION

How can you save money if you have a car and cannot use public transportation, a bicycle, or walk?

- Choose a location with better transit options, bike lanes, and walkways.
- Carpool with others.
- Run more errands in a single trip.
- Explore alternative methods of transportation without a car. Plan to sell or give up your car.

What About Walking?
Some People Say This:

I don't want to walk; it takes too much time, or it might be hot, cold, raining, or have bad weather, so I'm not even going to consider doing it. It's a waste of time, and time is money.

. . .

And Other People Say This:

I walk 3-5 miles a day. The benefits include the following:

I save money on healthcare because exercise reduces the chance of getting heart disease, cancer, diabetes, and strokes, and

I get fresh air, sunshine, aromas from flowers, and

I meet people and find out about healthcare, housing, food, and transport, and

I find out about community groups I can volunteer for and

If I share my goals with them, they get excited and want to help me, and

I get social activity, so I don't feel lonely, and

I find out about extraordinary events in the neighborhood, and

Began to realize I am not alone, and now everything has changed, and

All I have to do is shut up, listen, and be open.

What About Bicycling?
Some People Say This.

Bicycling is too dangerous. Car drivers don't care about people on bikes. There are no bike lanes, making it unsafe, especially when big trucks and buses are on the road.

Other People Say This.

. . .

Bicycling is a dangerous activity, but by being careful, I've reduced the chances of an accident.

Many cities have many bike lanes, but you must make an effort to find them.

Riding a bicycle is exhilarating, energizing, and fun.

In heavy traffic, I can bicycle to a destination faster than a car.

I have more freedom because I don't have to worry about a car all day.

I am closer to nature; I feel the sun, wind, rain, and the beauty of the Earth.

If I follow the rules and slow down, I minimize the chance of an accident.

If I'm going slower and am in an accident, I will likely have less damage than if I'm in a car accident.

In Germany, many people, including older individuals, use bicycles. The streets are designed to minimize traffic danger and provide advantages to people who bicycle, walk, and use public transit.

What About Transit?

Some People Say This.

Transit takes too long. I'm not waiting all day for the bus, and when it does come, it is very slow. Why would I be so stupid as to ride a bus?

Other People Say This.

. . .

Transit may take longer than driving a car, unless you factor in the time spent making money to pay for the car, fixing it, cleaning it, and covering all other expenses. Instead of paying to move a car, I prefer walking, bicycling, or using transit.

If I learn the process, I can use transit efficiently.

Many transit systems work well, but just like driving a car, it takes time to learn.

My stress level goes down when I'm not driving a car.

In transit, I can relax, eat, sleep, and look at the world.

Transit is less expensive than buying, fixing, and disposing of a car.

Since I don't have a car, I have more time and money, which allows me to take transit.

I have more time, energy, and money, and I don't have to worry about the car day and night.'

The Following Books By Dan Paul Help People Advance Their Transportation.

Click on the blue text link below to buy the book on Amazon.

Auto Free Design

Auto Free Design

Auto Free USA

Auto Free USA

CHAPTER 5
FOOD

You are what you eat. Would you rather be a dead piece of meat or a flower?

How Can We Save Money And Eat Good Food?

Grow your food.
Eat whole foods.
Eat wild plants.
Eat food people don't want.
Eat for nutrition, not superstition.

Eat Whole Foods.

Oranges, apples, carrots, broccoli, nettles, and wild berries are all whole foods. Soda pop, chips, candy, and cold cuts are all processed foods. Many fruits, vegetables, and beans are lower in cost per pound than processed foods. Some processed foods, such as olive oil, tofu, and hummus, are good for you.

. . .

Eat Wild Plants

Eating wild plants requires effort to find safe, nutritious ones and learn how to process and eat them. Start with the easy ones and approach it like a hobby. As I have time, I will discover one, two, or three more plants. Wild plants offer a unique nutritional profile that is not found in other plants. Each plant is unique. Adaptation is beneficial. Using plants with unique compounds may advance adaptation. Wild plantain grows in frigid climates. People step on it, and it grows right back. It is very tough and adaptive. Compare that to a monoculture crop, which requires all the perfect conditions to grow properly. The farmer must prepare the soil, plant the seeds at the exact right time, pray for good weather, and then, after months of waiting, take meticulous care to harvest the crop properly. Eating wild plants can boost your energy, vitality, and immune system, and it costs no money, time, or energy to grow the plant; you harvest it. It is as free as free gets.

Eat Food People Don't Want

Nearly everyone is picky about the food they eat. People don't shovel down a bunch of dirt down their throat. A lot of good food is thrown out every day. Getting food from a garbage can or dumpster can help you reduce the cost of eating. Others and I have done this for decades, with few problems. (This writing is not advice; it is a report.) People throw out a wide variety of food. We have eaten this food many times without any problems.

Eat For Nutrition

Some people eat to enjoy the taste of something delicious. Now, everyone loves delicious food, but what if the price tag is years of suffering and a short lifespan? Is it still worth it? What does eating for nutrition mean?

- -Adopt a new way to decide what food to eat.
- -Think about the power of plant nutrition to empower you to reach your goals.
- -Diverse nutrition generates peak performance
- -Diverse nutrition fortifies the systems of your body.
- -Learn to appreciate other flavors and textures.

Just Keep Investing

Now that you saved all that money, it's time to invest it. Use your mind to decide how to manage your money. If you view your money as an opportunity, take a risk and see what happens, you may achieve a return on your investment. In the following chapters, we will focus on investing your money. The book assumes that investing can be a way to view spending that offers advantages for the reader. That is why the author is using the term 'investing'.

CHAPTER 6
HEALTHCARE TAKE ACTION FOREVER

Refer to "Workers' Health Handbook, Save Your Life, Prevent Hospital Use, and Universal Health Care System" by Dan Paul for additional assistance with healthcare.

How can I invest money in healthcare?

When I invest my money, I expect a return on the investment. Is there any investment that could bring a higher return than an investment in my healthcare? By investing in my health, I can avoid costly medical bills and increase my income. I am proactive, and I can develop habits that help me avoid unnecessary use of the healthcare system. Can I budget for healthcare? If I have no money, I can invest my time and energy.

. . .

How Can I Advance My Healthcare If I Have No Money?

-I can eat free wild food that has medicinal value.

-Develop healthy eating, exercise, and sleeping habits to minimize the need for healthcare.

-I can make a plan to make money to spend on healthcare.

-I can make goals when I leave home to return home in good health.

What Are Good Healthcare Investments?

Investments that promote healthy habits, such as setting daily exercise goals.

If you wait long enough, you can find most items for free.

Find free or low-cost high-value healthcare insurance plans.

Find free or low-cost tools to fix your shelter in ways that improve your health.

Find free or buy used sporting equipment that you know you will use.

Find free or buy used, high-quality cookware, such as a cast-iron pan or stainless steel pot.

Learning how to identify and use wild and medicinal plants.

Invest your time in learning how to maintain your health.

. . .

The Following Books By Dan Paul Help People Advance Their Transportation.

Click on the blue text link below to buy the book on Amazon.

Workers Health Handbook

Workers Health Handbook

Save Your Life Prevent Hospital Use

Save Your Life Prevent Hospital Use

CHAPTER 7
HOUSING ACTION INVESTING

Refer to "Housing in the Danger Zone" and "Landlords and Tenants Against Eviction" by Dan Paul for more great ideas.

How Can I Invest In Housing?

- have no money. What do I do?
- Make goals for your housing. These are examples of housing goals:
- I want to have a place to live within the next three months.
- I plan to purchase a dilapidated house and renovate it within the next five years.
- I will join a coop in 6 months and solve all my housing problems.

Other Ways To Solve Your Housing Problems Without Money.

. . .

Volunteer to help someone do construction work to learn to fix your building.

Make plans to get housing. Ask other people to help you figure out the problem.

Tell everyone you know you are looking for housing. What do they recommend?

I Have Money, But I Need to Invest Less in Housing.

If you make more money, you are investing a smaller percentage of your income in housing.

If you live in market-rate housing, a coop can be a good investment.

Buy a fixer-upper house and renovate it. Caution: This will generate many problems.

Move in with other people. You will need to be flexible and practice good etiquette.

Money spent to bring a building up to code may be your best investment.

Always prioritize investing in repairs that keep the building up to code.

Fixing up junker buildings to code often yields the highest returns on your investment.

Find people with a bedroom, house, or apartment they don't use and offer to trade whatever you can offer, like your skills, for a place to live. Then save the money to buy a fixer-upper house. Tell people this is what you want to do. They may offer you a home or a deal on one.

When you help someone, ask them if they will sign a document that outlines the assistance you provided. Ask for a photo to document the work. Gather many of these and use them to establish and maintain your credibility with other people.

The Following Books By Dan Paul Help People Advance Their Housing.

Landlords and Tenants Against Eviction
Landlords and Tenants Against Eviction

Housing in the Danger Zone
Housing in the Danger Zone

CHAPTER 8
EDUCATION INVESTING IN EDIFICATION

Education may function well if it's guided by a goal. I need to focus my education on what I need here, now, and in the future. I'm investing my time, energy, and money in what I need.

How Can I Invest In My Education If I Have No Money?

- Make goals. Goals are free, but realizing them requires effort.
  Goals = results + time + budget.
  Ask others how to solve your problem.

Here Are Some Examples Of Goals I Will Educate Myself To Accomplish.

- I aim to double my monthly income in six months, but my current budget is zero.
- I aim to generate a passive income that covers double my monthly expenses within 2 to 5 years. Budget is zero.
- I will take the time to master the skills and reap the benefits in the future. Budget is zero.
- I will help five people do something today. Budget is zero?

Now repeat the process with different numbers in the budget. I will double my monthly income in 6 months. I have a budget of $500. What will I spend the money on?

Use the Internet and artificial intelligence to guide you to your goals. Try different methods and ideas. Write down your goals and discuss them with everyone. Tell them you are working it day and night, and you are looking for a mentor or mastermind group to help make it happen. Ask if they know anyone who might be interested in joining your group.

CHAPTER 9
TRANSPORTATION PEOPLE POWER INVESTING

Need a Vehicle, but I Don't Have the Money.
Make a plan with goals.

- I will walk, bicycle, or take transit to all destinations within 6 months to a year.
- I will make a list of benefits for my health, housing, transport, and food.
- I will create a plan to adjust my approach based on the results and feedback.

Can I eliminate trips I make with a vehicle?

Can I walk, bicycle, or ride transit?

Can I move to a location with transit and bike lanes?

What are the challenges in terms of income, housing, and education?

I Make A List Of Trips That I Make Each Week, Including:

- Income
- healthcare
- housing
- education
- food
- family
- friends
- entertainment

What trips can I make by walking? Bicycling? Using transit. What would it take to stop using a vehicle? I will gain advantages as I realize I don't need your vehicle.

Can I ride a roller skate, bicycle, or use an electric scooter to and from transit?

I Want To Live Without A Car. Where Should I Go?

Most cities have areas where people can live without a vehicle. Usually, the more people who walk, the less they need a car. Most cities have higher-density zoning. Zoning determines how land can be used. Zoning classifications include commercial, residential, industrial, governmental, and others. Higher-density areas provide housing and zoning for more people to live in a smaller area. Sometimes, if you see many buildings larger than 4 or 5 stories, the region may have transit, bike lanes, and sidewalks. Often, these are set up so that people can live without a car. A person can easily get to work, healthcare, education, and grocery stores without a vehicle.

Auto Free USA (Book By Dan Paul)

A movement is growing to liberate people from the oppressive conditions of auto use. Many cities are moving in that direction. They expand transit, bike lanes, and walkways to allow people to travel without the burden and danger of using an automobile.

Goals

- I want to get to work, healthcare, housing, and education.
- I want to do this safely and sustainably.
- Learn to use transit sustainably.

How to Get Rid of Your Car

The following table can help you live without a vehicle. Make a list of all the trips you take and put them in the 1st column. Put an x in the column of the way you get to your destination. For each trip you make with your car, draw an arrow to show an alternative route. The goal is to create a plan for making all trips without a car. If you practice making all trips without a car for a couple of months, you can sell or give away your vehicle, bring it to a junkyard, and be free of all the misery indefinitely.

Transit Table

This Transit Table provides a way to organize a transition from using an automobile to using other methods of transport, including walking, bicycling, and using transit. The idea is to walk, bicycle, or use transit to move between destinations.

Transit Table

Destination	Walk	Bicycle	Transit	Car
Work				
Healthcare				
Education				
Bank				
Food				
Fun				

Transit Table Instructions: Fill out this table. In the car column, draw an arrow (red, yellow, or green) to the walk, bicycle, or transit to design a life free from a car. Make a plan and take action. It may take time; you may have to fail five times, but without taking action, you will not reap the benefits.

Use red, yellow, and green to designate the amount of interest. Red is no interest, yellow is maybe, and green is go, so you would have to work the most on the red marks and transition from yellow to green. Once you get the green, you should realize your goals and benefits

CHAPTER 10
WHOLE AND WILD FOOD

We spend money on food, which can be seen as an investment. If the food is an investment, it has a specific goal. One goal is to live a long and healthy life, for example, 80 years. What foods will lead to that result? Assuming we would use non-processed, vegan whole foods, what would those be?

Standard investments at the grocery store include;

- Vegetables: Carrots, potatoes, onions, greens.
- Fruit: Apples, oranges, bananas, grapes, raisins.
- Legumes: lentils, beans, tofu, tempeh, seeds.
- Nuts: peanuts, walnuts, almonds, and hazelnuts (also known as filberts).
- Fish: sardines, herring, fish with oil.
- Processed foods, such as tofu, olive oil, and apple cider vinegar, are generally considered healthy.
- Avoid sugar, soda, candy, chips, and most animal products.

Wild Food

Wild food requires some time and labor to set up, but it is nearly free. You want to find areas that are free from dog waste, herbicides, pesticides, and other chemicals. Yes, I know that doesn't exist, but do the best you can. Finding a patch of wild greens is a great find, usually common in the country, but it is more often cultivated. It's a fun habit. If you have a phone, download and use a software program like iNaturalist or PlantNet to identify plants. Most plants are edible and medicinal, but you won't know unless you ask people and study. Since few people are doing it, there may be an abundance. Wild plants can provide peak nutrition that is uncommon in the marketplace. Some compounds are found only in one plant or a single family of plants. This is a great hobby to share with your friends and family. As you become familiar with the plants and utilize them, you will feel empowered.

ABOUT THE AUTHOR

Dan Paul grew up picking rocks, going fishing, and building houses in Lake Wobegon. For decades, he worked on the most sustainable projects. With a degree in sustainable transport and development and years of experience working on alternative projects, such as Dreamtime Village, Bolozone, and the Urbana Indymedia project, a community has embarked on a journey to end the dictatorship of capitalism.

ALSO BY DAN PAUL

Series: Philosophy of Action, Design, and Multiplicity

Book 1: Auto Free Design

Book 2: Workers' Health Handbook

Book 3: Save Your Life: Prevent Hospital Use

Book 4: Coop Owners' Handbook

Book 5: Eye on AI: Meeting Needs Sustainably

Book 6: Travels on the Nomadic Terrain

Book 7: Tales of the Urban Shaman

Book 8: Housing in the Danger Zone

Book 9: Corona Time

Book 10: Philosophy of Design, Action, and Multiplicity

Other Books By Dan Paul

Landlords and Tenants Against Eviction

Auto Free USA

AI Frankenstein: Concise, Critical, Common Sense Artificial Intelligence

Universal Voting System

Forever Flowers: Requiem in the Land of Milk and Honey

Universal Basic Income

Blueprint to Reverse Climate Change

Websites:

https://viaradmedia.org/wp

https://autofreedesign.com

http://workershealthhandbook.com

http://sylphu.com

Social Media:

https://www.facebook.com/profile.php?id=61555599616489

https://twitter.com/jonblu

https://www.instagram.com/jonblu61/

The ollowing books were written by Dan Paul. These are the first five books in a series called Philosophy of Action Design and Multiplicity.

Auto Free Design

Workers Health Handbook

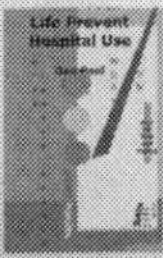

Save Your Life Prevent Hospital Use

Coop Owners Manual

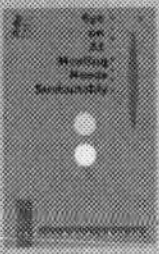

Eye on AI Meeting Needs Sustainably

The following books were written by Dan Paul. These are the second five books (5-10) in a series called Philosophy of Action Design and Multiplicity.

Travels on the Nomadic Terrain

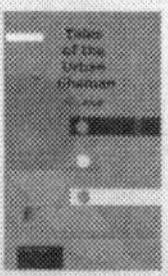

Tales of the Urban Shaman

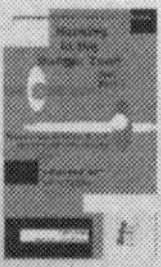

Housing in the Danger Zone

Corona Time

Philosophy of Design, Action, and Multiplicity

The following books were written by Dan Paul.
Auto Free USA
AI Frankstein Concise, Critical, Common Sense Artificial Intelligence
Universal Voting System
Forever Flowers Requiem in the Land of Milk and Honey
Universal Basic Income

These books were written by Dan Paul.

Blueprint to Reverse Climate Change

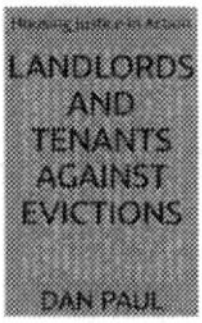

Landlords and Tenants Against Eviction

Made in the USA
Monee, IL
09 November 2026

67380379R00034